Linda Sonntag

The Leprechaun Library
published by
G.P. PUTNAM'S SONS
NEW YORK

MAN'S BEST FRIEND

Be kind and tender to the Frog,
And do not call him names,
As 'Slimy skin', or 'Polly-wog',
Or likewise 'Ugly James',
Or 'Gape-a-grin', or 'Toad-gone-wrong',
Or 'Billy Bandy-knees':
The Frog is justly sensitive
To epithets like these.
No animal will more repay
A treatment kind and fair;
At least so lonely people say
Who keep a frog (and, by the way,
They are extremely rare).

HILAIRE BELLOC

Frog Carnival

At the end of February each year, carnivals are held in many Dutch towns. Though the origins of the celebration are pagan, dating from Roman times, its purpose is to give people an excuse to over-indulge in food and drink before the abstinence of the Lenten season.

Each carnival-town elects a Prince of Fools, who is chosen by a council of eleven men – 'the Council of Fools' – for an annual term of office. Besides raising money for charity, his main responsibility is to see that people enjoy the carnival.

At carnival time one town, s'Hertogenbosch, the capital of the province of North Brabant, even changes its name: It becomes 'Oeteldonk', which means 'the Place of Frogs'. Here, the Prince of Fools is given the honorary title of Frog Prince. During the three days of revels he is given complete freedom in the town and goes around, like a medieval Lord of Misrule, encouraging normally sober citizens to eat and drink more than is good for them. The town itself is festooned with pictures of frogs which appear on flags and posters, while people sport frog motifs on their clothing.

The town's enthusiasm for frogs, two of which can be seen incorporated into its coat of arms, is thought to have originated centuries ago when the region had a very large frog population. They are not so numerous today but the frog festival still endures.

THE FROG PRINCE

Once upon a time there was a beautiful princess. Every day she played outside with a golden ball. However, one day she dropped the ball and it fell down a deep well. The princess began to weep, but a voice at her feet croaked, 'Stop crying, princess.' She looked down and saw a frog. He promised to fetch her ball if, in return, she would let him share her food and her bed. The princess agreed unhesitatingly, so the frog dived into the well, emerged with the golden ball in his mouth and placed it at the princess's feet.

The princess forgot all about the frog until the next day when he appeared in the royal dining-room. She tried to ignore him, but the king, hearing of her promise, told her that she must not break it. She lifted the frog on to the table and he ate from her plate, but the princess could not swallow a morsel.

Then he said, 'Now let's go to bed.' The princess was horrified, but her father said she must keep her promise. Holding the frog between her thumb and forefinger she went up to her room. Once she was in bed, he hopped up on to her pillow. The princess, overcome with revulsion, dashed the ugly creature against the wall.

To her astonishment it was a handsome prince who picked himself up from the floor. The princess had broken a witch's evil spell. The pair fell instantly in love, were married, and lived happily ever after.

FROG SYMBOLS

The frog is a symbol of fruitfulness.

The Egyptian goddess Hekt has the head of a frog. She symbolizes the embryonic state of the grain which, having died and decomposed, begins to germinate again. She is one of the midwives who assists each morning at the birth of the sun.

In dreams, frogs signify indiscretion.

To American Indians, Australian aborigines and Hindus the frog is the melancholy croaker who heralds the coming of rain. In India his croaking is compared to the chanting of sacred rites.

In Burma, an amulet shaped like a frog and fashioned in amber or gold is worn by children to protect them from the Evil Eye.

In Japan the frog is called *kawazu* and is symbolic of energy and perseverance.

In Altai Tartar mythology the frog discovered the mountain bearing birch and stones from which the first fire was made. Hence he is the bringer of fire to man.

Frogs are said to be the souls of children who have died. To kill one is unlucky.

FROGS IN ART

From early times people have represented the world around them in art and it is no surprise to find that the ubiquitous frog has been used very frequently as a source of inspiration.

The ancient Peruvians placed frog statuettes in their tombs to remind the dead souls of the world they had left behind. The Quinbaya Indians of Colombia, who revered all creatures living in lakes and ponds, made clay drinking vessels on which they depicted frogs. The Romans incorporated frogs in their mosaics, and one example found in Naples shows a very contented frog sitting on a lily pad. The Chinese made netsukes, the ivory ornaments which they hung from their sword belts, in the form of frogs.

The artistic appeal of frogs continues into this century. Carl Fabergé, jeweller to the Imperial Russian Court, incorporated a frog into a parasol handle. This frog has diamond eyes set in gold. He is carved out of jade, climbing up a translucent green enamelled column; the whole handle is only $4\frac{1}{2}$ inches high. Tiffany's, the New York jewellers, commissioned an extraordinary inkwell on which four ivory jewelled frogs crouched to support the inkwell's lid.

Contemporary artists are still fascinated by frogs. One potter, Anthony Bennett, has been inspired by the many textures and colours of frogs. Developing the uncanny potential of the frog to metamorphize into human shapes, he has made many frog jugs. Looking at these, it is difficult to know where the frog ends and the man begins. Among his other creatures are larger-than-life realistic frogs – some as large as 24 inches wide and 19 inches high – who sit gleaming on pottery stones.

HOW MEN WERE TURNED INTO FROGS

Juno, the Queen of the Gods, was so jealous of her beauty that she barred the goddess Leto from settling anywhere in the world. Poor Leto had barely recovered from giving birth to twins when Juno condemned her again to her wanderings.

With her babes at her breast and her milk sucked dry, Leto was parched with thirst as she staggered on under the scorching Lycian sun. Then she came to a lake where some peasants were gathering reeds. She knelt down to drink, but they tried to shoo her away. She begged them for water, if only for her

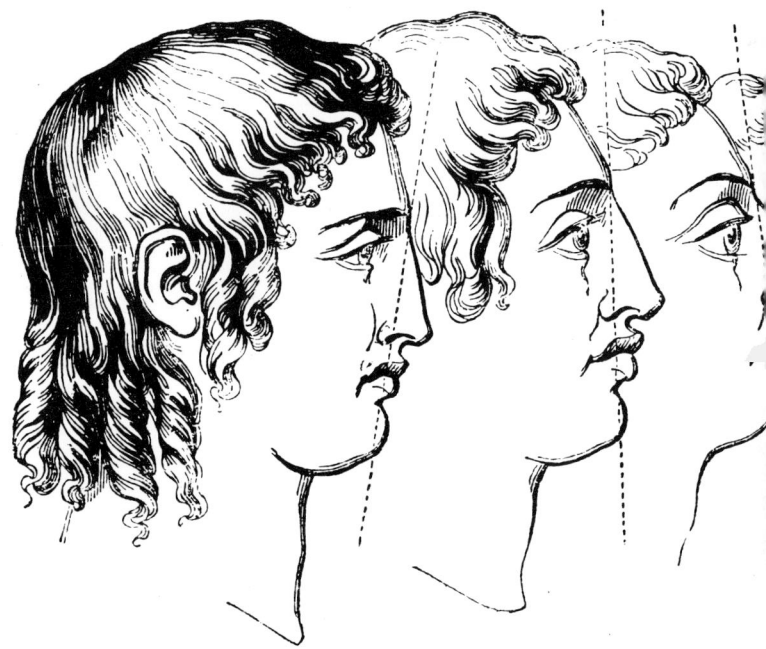

babes. At this the peasants became even more unpleasant, muddying the lake's water with their hands and feet. Leto raised her despairing eyes to the heavens and cried: 'Live then forever in that lake of yours.'

At this the peasants suddenly submerged themselves in the lake, leaving only their heads on the surface. Their voices became strangely harsh. Their throats puffed and their mouths gaped wider as they continued their abuse. Their eyes bulged and their necks seemed to disappear into their shoulders. Their backs turned green while their bellies remained white. They had changed into frogs!

OVID: METAMORPHOSES

CHINESE FROGS

The Chinese think highly of the frog. They have given it the honorary title of Heavenly Chicken, and tell how its spawn falls from the sky with the dew. They set frog statuettes in their paddy fields, hoping for plenty of rain. But the Chinese frog is not always a benevolent animal. It is known to lend its shape to the evil spirit which swallows the moon, thus causing an eclipse. An ancient legend tells of another link between the frog and the moon.

Once, long ago, the handsome Chinese warrior Huo I fell in love with a beautiful water-sprite who lived in the Lo river. Huo I was so jealous of the sprite's husband, the god of the Yellow River, that he killed him. Threatened with death for this deed, Huo I persuaded the Great Goddess of the Western Skies to give him the gift of immortality. She presented him with a pill which she said would bring him everlasting life. Huo I was so relieved that instead of taking the pill, he put it in a golden casket and gave it to his wife, Chang O, to look after. Chang O then saw her chance for revenge. As soon as he left the house the next day, Chang O went to the place where the pill was hidden and swallowed it. When Huo I returned and discovered it was gone, he fell into a deadly fury and chased Chang O to the ends of the earth to get his revenge. When he had all but caught up with her, Chang O raised her arms to the sky in desperation saying, 'I have nowhere to turn to; where can I hide?' In an instant she was turned into a frog and with one spring she leaped up on to the moon and took refuge in a palace of gold. There she has lived ever since, and there she will stay for all eternity.

FROGS IN LARGE NUMBERS

Today there are some 1,200 known frog species in the world, and the frog is probably the most numerous of all animals. Not only are there a lot of them but frogs have the dubious distinction of being the first creatures on earth to develop a voice – hence their Latin name *rana*, which means 'noise'.

Plagues of frogs have been recorded since the dawn of time, and perhaps the best-known is the biblical plague of frogs, in which the frogs came up from the river Nile and covered the land of Egypt. They came into the houses, into the kitchens – even the bedrooms – and covered all the people. At last the plague subsided. 'And they gathered them together upon heaps: and the land stank.' (Exodus : 8; 14).

However, there is plenty of evidence that, given certain conditions, frogs do appear in their millions. In South Africa recently a plague of frogs in a railway cutting caused the train to grind to a halt. But the way they appear is no longer a mystery. Frogs do not fall out of the sky. Neither are they whirled through the ether by cyclones.

What happens is this. Given three or four good wet seasons when the veldt is lush, green and full of plump grasshoppers and plenty of rainwater to keep tadpoles refreshed in their pools, frogs will multiply rapidly. At the first hint of dry weather, however, they fill themselves up with water and burrow underground. (In Australia aborigines dig up these frogs for water in times of drought.) A sudden heavy rainfall will penetrate the frogs' hideout and bring them back to the surface in large numbers. A person emerging from shelter after heavy rains to see hordes of frogs where there were none before cannot be blamed for thinking it might have 'rained frogs'.

THE AMOROUS FROG

There are many versions of the popular folk song 'A frog he would a-wooing go', which is well-loved in both Britain and America, where it is known as 'Frog went a-courting'.

Mr Frog lived in a well. Though his mother had warned him against going a-courting, a certain Miss Mouse had caught his eye and captured his heart ('Hey ho,' says Rowley!) and he was determined to ask for her paw in marriage. So he took himself off to the mill in which she lived and, on bended knee, he proposed. Miss Mouse replied, somewhat haughtily:

> 'Not without the Rat's consent
> I wouldn't marry the President.'

Fortunately, the Rat was delighted at the proposal, as it seems he feared his niece would never be a bride. Accordingly, the gown was bought, the Weasel delivered the marriage banns and the wedding feast was arranged. Opinion is divided as to the food and drink provided and the guests invited. English versions have it that genteel portions of dogwood bark and sips of catnip tea were served, while in America's Deep South the happy couple and their friends feasted on 'two green beans and a black-eyed pea'. The guests vary according to region from a Negro and a black snake, a bug, a fly, a bee, a flea, a dog, a mare and a cow to (in Ireland) a snail playing the bagpipes.

But Frog and Mouse were never destined to live happily ever after. In most versions the guests end up rather the worse for wear (the fly dies, the tick is sick), but as for our hero and heroine, they fall victim to a duck and a cat and do not live to see another day – which all proves that Mother was right.

FROG BEAN-BAG

This friendly little frog bean-bag is simply made from two pieces of material sewn together and filled with rice. It can be made to sit up, cross its legs and generally take notice.

Materials A piece of material (e.g. green satin, cotton print) 16 × 20 inches (40 × 50 cm); thread; two large beads and twelve small beads for eyes; 4 oz (100 g) round-grain rice; paper, pencil and measure; tailor's chalk; scissors.

To make Make a paper pattern from diagram opposite, in which each square represents 1½ inches (4 cm). Cut out around outline of frog. Fold material to form a double thickness 8 × 10 inches (20 × 50 cm). Pin pattern to material and trace frog outline with tailor's chalk. Remove pattern and pinning material together, cut around chalk outline. Pin the two pieces of material right sides together. Allowing ¼ inch (5 mm) for the seam, tack around the outline leaving a gap of 2 inches (5 cm) at the base of the body. Machine around frog outline. If you do not have a machine, backstitch around the outline using double thread. Remove tacking and carefully turn frog right-side out. Use the blunt end of a knitting needle to turn out completely arms and legs. Fill the frog with rice using a piece of rolled paper as a funnel. Stitch up the gap by overstitching with single thread. Make the eyes by sewing one large bead surrounded by six small beads.

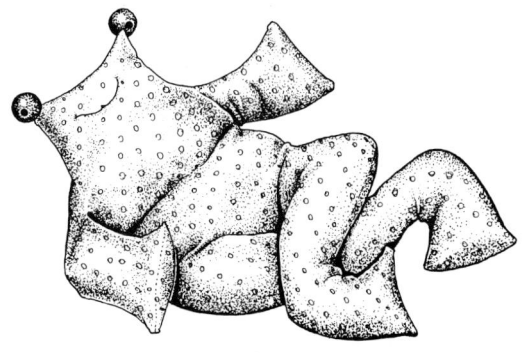

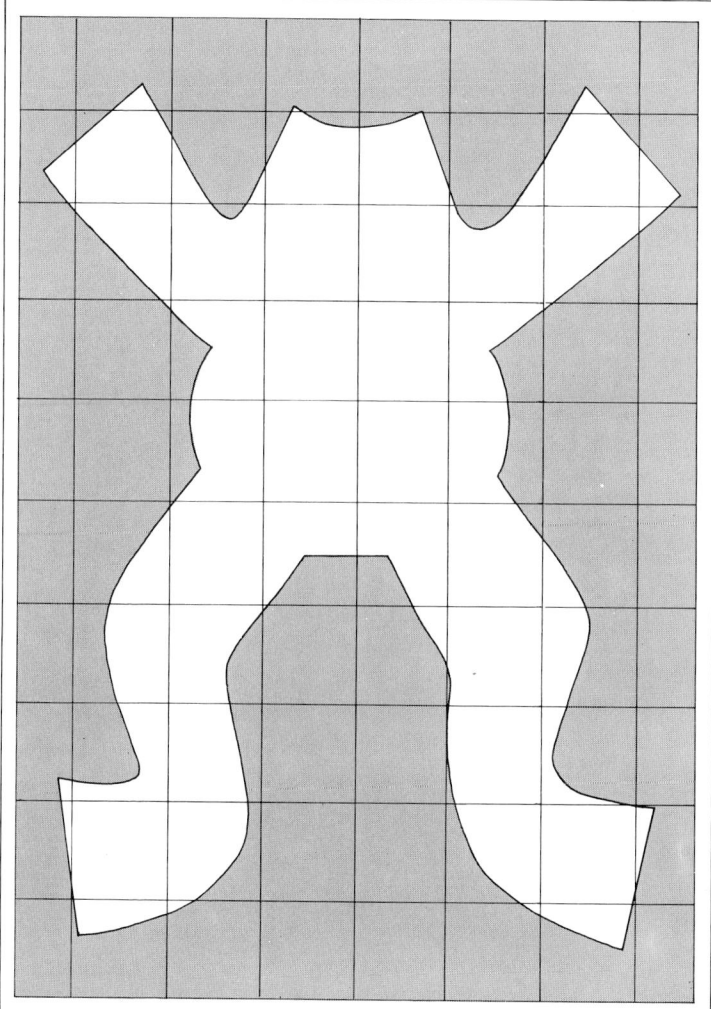

THE LAZY FROG

Once a frog and a hen shared a house. This frog was very lazy and left the hen to do all the work, sweeping the floor, cooking the food and collecting firewood. Every night the exhausted hen would say: 'Frog, tomorrow it is your turn to go and fetch wood for the fire.'

Every morning, the frog would wake up when the sun was already high in the sky and refuse to do his small share of the work. His excuse was always the same: 'I can't go and collect wood now. Have you ever seen a frog out in the sun?' Yet, all the same, he would amble off to find some shady place in which to laze away the day. He would return to the house when all the work was done and just as the food was prepared.

The hen grew more and more exasperated with the slothful frog. Then one day her problem was solved. As he was dozing on a damp stone among tall bullrushes, a hawk circling in the sky above, caught sight of the plump frog. Sweeping down, he snatched up the frog, devouring him before the frog had a chance to realize what was happening. The hen was delighted, for now she had the house to herself.

HAUSA FOLKTALE

GRENOUILLES GASTRONOMIQUES

Frogs' legs are well known to be a speciality of French cuisine. There are four types of frog commonly found in France which can be used in the kitchen. These are the green frog, the common frog, the rusty frog and the mute frog. The best and most expensive frogs of all come from Solonge and Dombes and are prized for their delicate flesh and subtle taste. Yet strangely enough, most of the frogs consumed in France today are imported from Central Europe because these are plumper and more muscular than French ones.

To prepare a frog

Skin the frog, and discard all but the legs, the only edible part. Skewer the legs and immerse in very cold water. Change the water every two hours to whiten the flesh. Dry and cook. Allow three pairs of legs per person.

Grenouilles à l'anglaise

Prepare the frogs' legs as above. Season, dip in beaten egg, coat with breadcrumbs and fry lightly till golden.

THE COALMINER AND THE FROG

In Poland Skarbnik, the spirit of the coalmines, watches over the miners and brings them luck. One day Skarbnik was following a group of miners to the pit when a young fellow called Bombas began to taunt Adam, an old man who walked ahead because he never found any coal. The old man said nothing, for after all it was true. He had worked in the mines since his youth, but all he had uncovered was earth and stones.

Skarbnik decided to help. He turned himself into a big green frog and hopped down the mine. Bombas, seeing him first, raised his shovel to squash the creature, but Adam picked up the frog and put it in his jacket. When it was time to eat, he offered it a share of his dry bread, upon which the frog led him to a new rich seam of coal. Adam was delighted and gave the frog half his wages.

He told his wife what had happened and they decided to invite the frog and all their friends to dinner. Adam's wife prepared a rich meal and when all the guests were seated they toasted the frog in vodka and congratulated Adam on his good fortune.

Suddenly the door opened and there stood Bombas: 'Aren't I good enough to be invited?' he sneered, and, walking up to the head of the table, he kicked the frog's chair from under him. All the lamps went out and the room was filled with a strange light. On the frog's chair the word SKARBNIK was spelled out in silver coins. Everyone then realized that this had been no ordinary frog.

From that day on, Adam always earned a good wage in the mines, but Bombas lived in constant fear lest Skarbnik should take his revenge.

THE FROGS CHOOSE A KING

In days gone by frogs lived in glorious liberty in lakes, ponds and streams and were subject to no one. By and by they got tired of their free and easy life and asked Jupiter to send them a king to teach them the difference between good and evil, to punish them for their crimes and reward them for their good deeds. Jupiter, scornful of their foolishness, cast a log out of the heavens and told them it was a king.

The log landed with an almighty splash in the lake and, in fear of their ruler, the frogs burrowed into the mud until one of them, braver than the rest, ventured forth and pronounced the king too tame.

The frogs immediately asked for a new king, and this time Jupiter sent them a fearsome beast. Some say the monarch was a serpent, and others claim that he was a stork. But on one matter there can be no disagreement: the king deprived his subjects of both their liberty and their property. When the frogs claimed that his rule was too strict, Jupiter replied: 'They that are not contented when they are well must be patient when things are amiss with them, and people had better rest where they are than go farther and fare worse.'

The moral of this tale is that the multitude will never be satisfied.

AESOP

FROGS AS PARENTS

Among over a thousand different species of frog it is not surprising to find that some frogs have bizarre breeding habits. Some frogs nurture their offspring in strange ways. The male Darwin's frog swallows the fertilized eggs and keeps them in his vocal sac. When the tadpoles develop and start squirming about, he spits them out. In one little-known African species, the eggs actually develop inside the female and froglets, not tadpoles, are born. The male African bullfrog will sit surrounded by his tadpoles, protecting them from predators.

Other frogs find strange places in which to lay their eggs. Waterlily frogs lay their eggs in a sandwich – between two lily leaves stuck together with albumen. Some treefrogs lay their eggs in dewdrops which form in the leaf axils of plants. The bush squeaker frog lays each of its thirty eggs beneath individual leaves on the forest floor.

Some frogs build their own special frog nurseries. The blacksmith frog moulds its own clay breeding ponds, while the kloof frog makes a jelly cake and the Gray treefrog fashions a nest of foam.

If the parents are peculiar, the offspring are no less odd. Rattray's frog lays its eggs in a hole in the ground some distance from water. Its tadpoles are so helpless that they drown if they fall into the parental pool. Other tadpoles are so aggressive that they happily turn cannibal and eat any of their unfortunate fully-grown brothers and sisters who return to the pond where they were born.

FROGS AND WITCHCRAFT

> Eye of newt, and toe of frog,
> Wool of bat, and tongue of dog,
> Adder's fork, and blind-worm's sting,
> Lizard's leg, and howlet's wing,
> For a charm of powerful trouble,
> Like a hell-broth boil and bubble.

These words are chanted by the witches in Shakespeare's play *Macbeth*. Indeed, no witch's brew is complete without the addition of some part of a frog. If you look at any illustration of a witch's coven or into a book of spells you will always find some reference to frogs.

For example, a frog can give you power over people. To achieve this, a live frog should be put into a perforated box and buried in a black ants' nest. When the ants have picked the bones clean, the skeleton is thrown into a running brook at midnight. All the bones will float away with the current, save one. This will travel mysteriously upstream. Once recovered, this bone will endow its owner with the power of controlling people – and also horses which have not been broken in. Warts will disappear, too, if you rub them with this magic bone.

However, some witchcraft did not always achieve the desired ends. One Italian lady in the sixteenth century wished to kill her husband. He had a weak heart and, knowing frogs were used in witchcraft, she boiled one up with his pottage. Her husband ate the dish and, contrary to all expectations, recovered. But then the wife did not know that there is a chemical substance in frog's skin which is a cure for heart failure.

FROGGY CURES

According to Pliny, the Roman naturalist, a frog is something that no first-aid box should be without. Alive or dead, boiled or reduced to ashes, frogs are an invaluable cure for all sorts of ailments. Here are some of his recommendations.

Toothache Boil the frog in vinegar and use the juice as a mouth-wash. If you object to the taste, suspend frogs by their hindlegs over boiling vinegar until their saliva drops into it. Use the resulting liquid as a gargle.

Arthritis Apply fresh frogs from time to time as required. They can be cut up before application if preferred.

Fevers Rub the patient with the grease of frogs boiled in oil at a place where three roads meet. Alternatively, drown the frogs in oil, rub the oil into the body and wear the frog under the clothing as an amulet.

Irritations of the skin Catch the frogs soon after birth (i.e. when still tadpoles) and reduce to ashes in a new earthenware vessel; then stuff the ash up the nostrils.

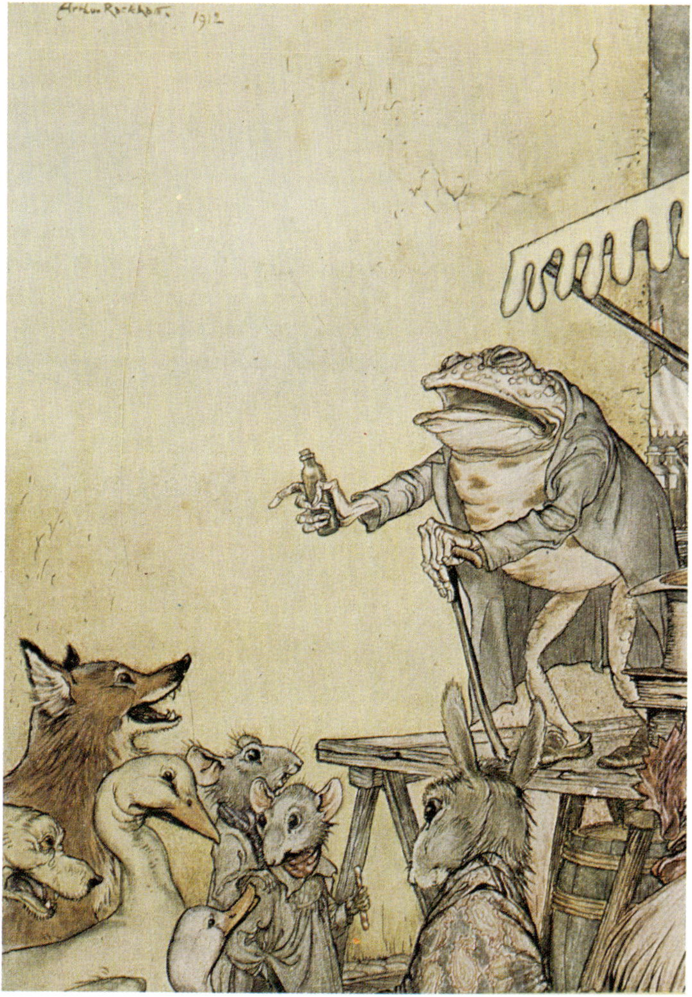
Arthur Rackham 1912

WHY THERE IS NO LIFE AFTER DEATH

One day the people of Togo got together to talk about life and death. They agreed unanimously that they did not want to die, but none of them was brave enough to go to God and ask for eternal life, so they decided to send a dog in their place.

The dog set off, but after he had gone only a little way he began to grow hungry. Soon he smelled a delicious aroma and followed his nose into a house where an old man was boiling a tasty soup.

Meanwhile, a frog who had overheard the discussion had set off, of his own accord, to tell God that men had decided they did not want to live again after death. As the dog was eating his soup he saw the frog hopping by, but the soup was so good he went on eating and did not pay any attention to the frog.

The frog reached God first, and God listened attentively to his request. When the dog came running in with his petition God declared himself embarrassed by the conflicting messages; but because the frog had arrived first, he allowed men to die and did not grant them eternal life.

TOGOLAND FOLKTALE

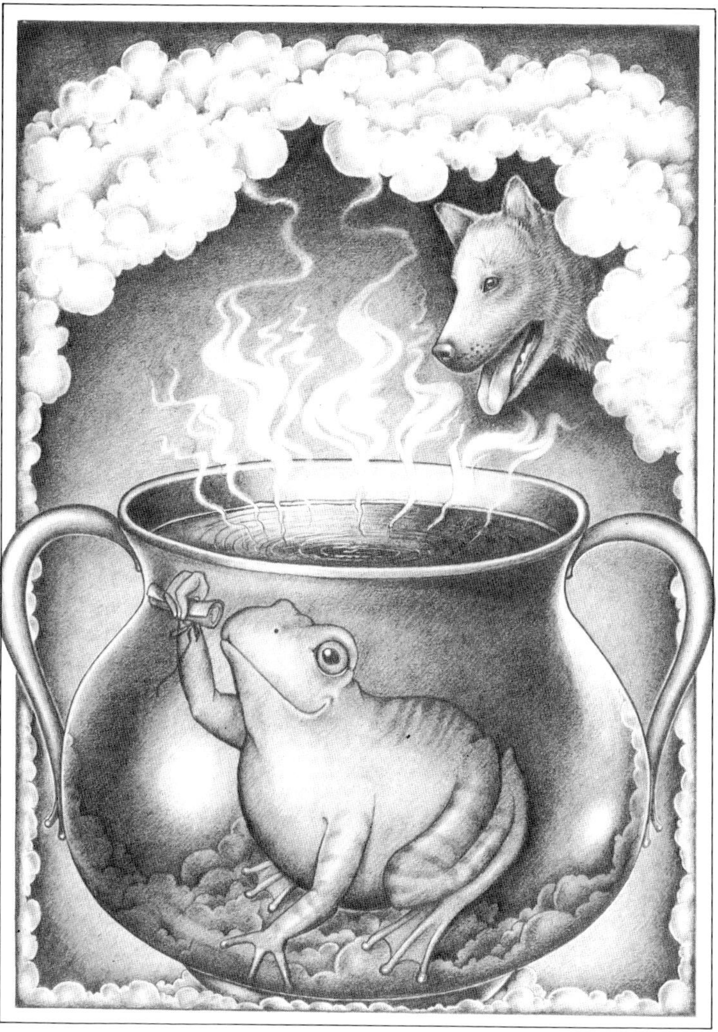

Frog Games

Leapfrog first became a popular game in the sixteenth century – Jan Breughel painted children indulging in this strange sport in 1560. In 1805 William Howitt, a teacher, recorded that the attraction of the game seemed to be growing. He observed his whole school – 180 pupils in all – leaping in a single line.

In the north of England, frog-in-the-middle is a more appropriate name for the age-old game usually known as piggy-in-the-middle. The 'frog' stands in the centre of a circle and has to leap in the air, arms outstretched, to intercept a flying object thrown between people on either side of him. An equally energetic frog game is the Frog Dance, a jig danced while crouched down like a frog.

'The Play of the wide-mouth waddling frog, to amuse the Mind and exercise the Memory' is a family game of questions and forfeits, similar to 'The Twelve Days of Christmas', rather less well known today than in Victorian times. The participants must commit to memory the following nonsense: 'A gaping wide-mouth waddling frog / Two pudding ends would choke a dog / Three monkeys tied to a clog / Four horses stuck in a bog / Five puppies by our dog's ball / Daily for their breakfast call / Six beetles against a wall / Close by an old woman's apple stall / Seven lobsters in a dish / As fresh as any heart could wish / Eight joiners in a joiners' hall / Working with their tools and all / Nine peacocks in the air / I wonder how they all came there / Ten comets in the sky / Some low and some high / Eleven ships sailing o'er the main / Some bound for France and some for Spain / Twelve huntsmen with horse and hounds / Hunting over other men's grounds.'

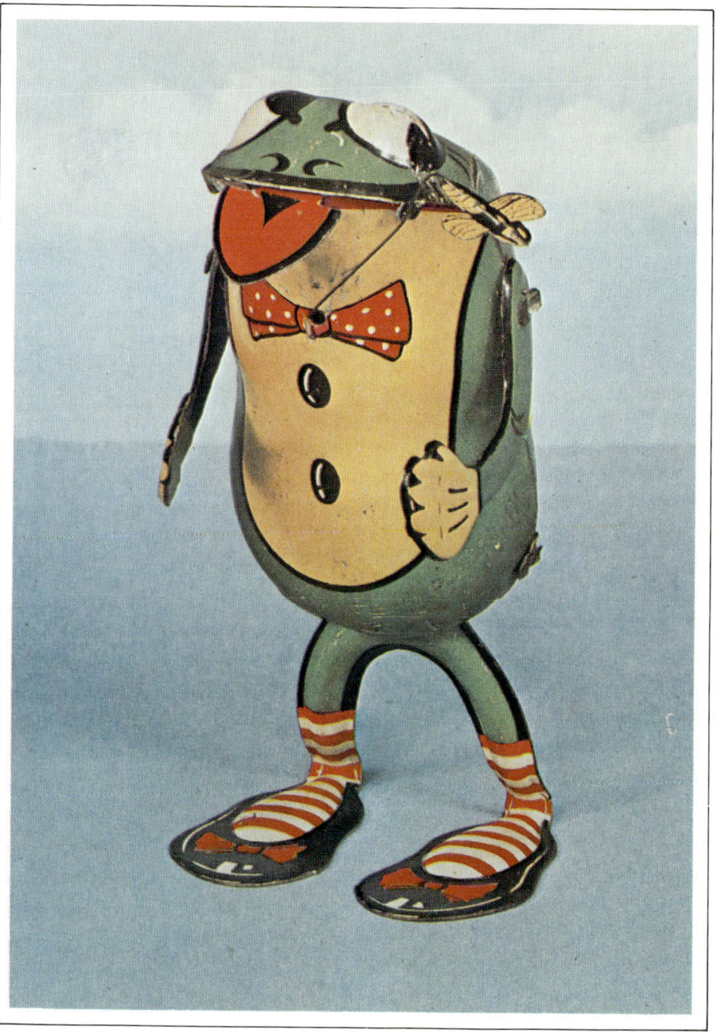

The Tale of Mr Jeremy Fisher

Beatrix Potter, the writer and artist, had a lifelong rapport with frogs. As a young girl she kept them as pets and even took them on holiday with her. When she was seventeen she wrote in her diary: 'Poor little Punch died on the 11th. Green frog, had him five or six years. He has been on extensive journeys.'

In 1892 she offered a series of ten frog drawings to Nisters, a German printer, at a price of 25 shillings. After a good deal of hard bargaining she managed to sell them for 22s 6d and they appeared in a children's annual under the title 'A Frog He Would A-fishing Go'. Twelve years later, when she had the idea for Mr Jeremy Fisher, she bought her drawings back for £6 and began to revise them. The urbane Mr Fisher, wearing close-fitting tights, dainty pumps, a starched collar and a bulging waistcoat under his practical mackintosh, sallies forth in his lily-leaf boat to catch a dish of minnows for his supper. Despite this debonaire appearance and impeccable equipment, consisting of a knapsack of butterfly sandwiches, a tough stalk of grass for a rod and a fine long white horse-hair as a line, he catches nothing but spiny Jack Sharp, the stickleback. Worse follows: his boat is overturned by a trout who proceeds to swallow the intrepid fisherman whole. Fortunately, his life is saved by his mackintosh – the trout finds its taste most disagreeable and spits him out, consuming only his galoshes. Mr Jeremy Fisher hurries home, having given up fishing for good, and serves his friends, Sir Isaac Newton and Alderman Ptolemy Tortoise, a warming dish of roast grasshopper with ladybird sauce.

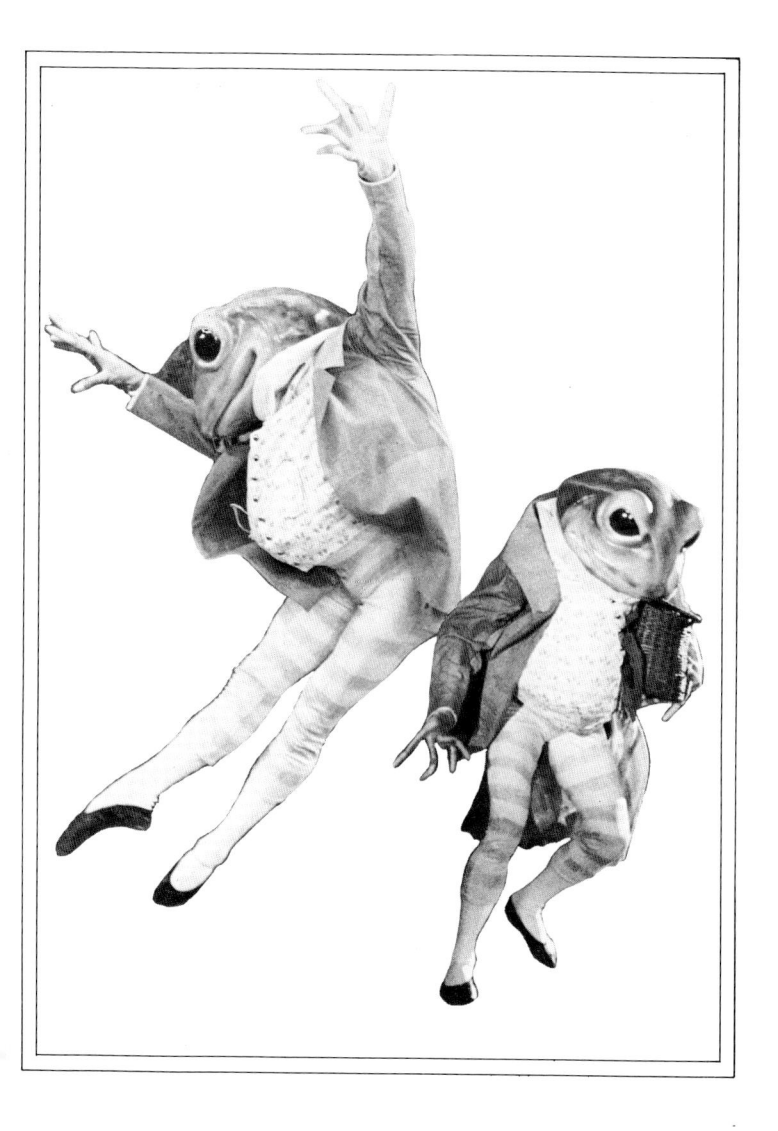

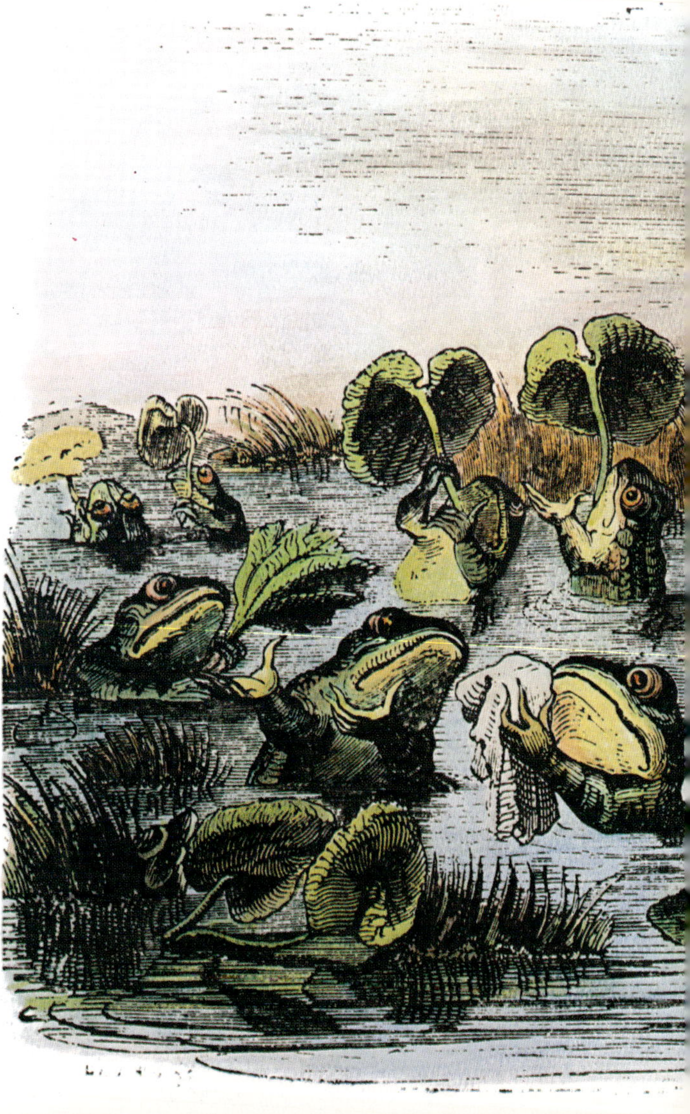

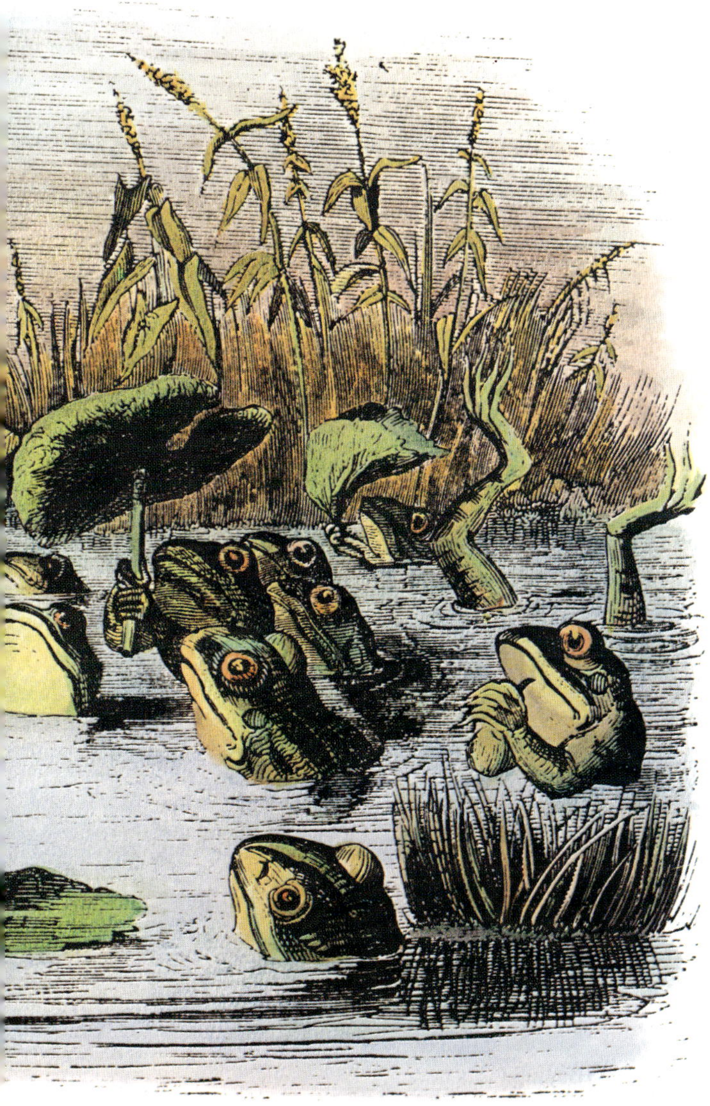

In the Service of Science

Over many centuries the anatomy of the frog has been more fully studied and described than that of any animal except man. Amongst the great scientists who have devoted themselves to this humble amphibian are Jan Swammerdam, William Harvey and Anton Leeuwenhoek. The latter once claimed with enthusiasm that his study of the frog's bloodstream 'has often-times been so recreating to me, that I do not believe that all the pleasure of fountains or waterworks, either natural or made by art, could have pleased my sight so well.'

Luigi Galvani, an eighteenth-century professor of medicine, is perhaps better known than these three. One day he was holding a class in his Bologna home when he was interrupted by a scream from the kitchen. His wife had borrowed his scalpel to skin a frog when the instrument fell from her grasp and impaled itself on the frog's thigh. The thigh, which was resting on a zinc plate, began to twitch violently as if alive. The professor was delighted and declared to his admiring audience that he had discovered the elemental force of life – animal electricity. Thereafter Galvani dedicated his life's work to frogs and became widely known for his experiments using frogs' legs as lightning conductors. He also gave science a new term: galvanism.

Sadly, his work was not as important as he supposed. It took a greater scientist, Alessandro Volta, to explain that what he had discovered was not the elemental life force, but simply an electrical conductor. The moist frog's leg had served to transmit an electrical current between the different metals of the scalpel and the plate.

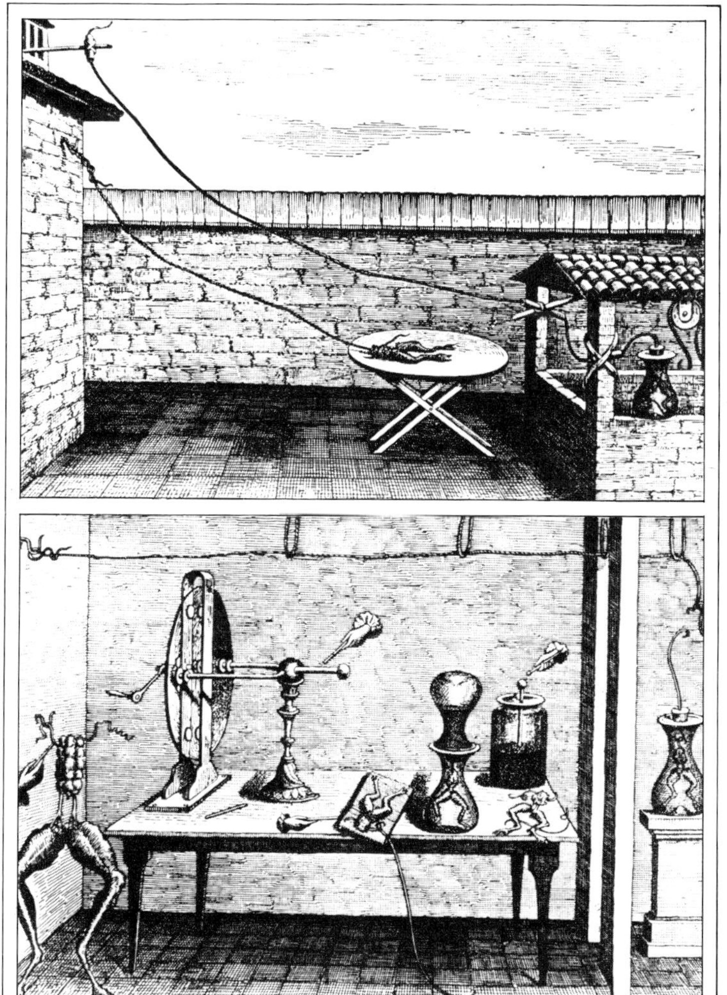

FROG SAYINGS

There are not frogs wherever there is water; but
Wherever there are frogs water will be found.

GOETHE

What are little boys made of?
What are little boys made of?
Frogs and snails
And puppy-dogs' tails
That's what little boys are made of.

ENGLISH NURSERY RHYME

Though boys throw stones at frogs in sport,
the frogs do not die in sport, but in earnest.

GREEK SAYING

The frog that has not seen the sea
Thinks the well a fine stretch of water.

JAPANESE PROVERB

The frog's own croak betrays him.

CHINESE SAYING

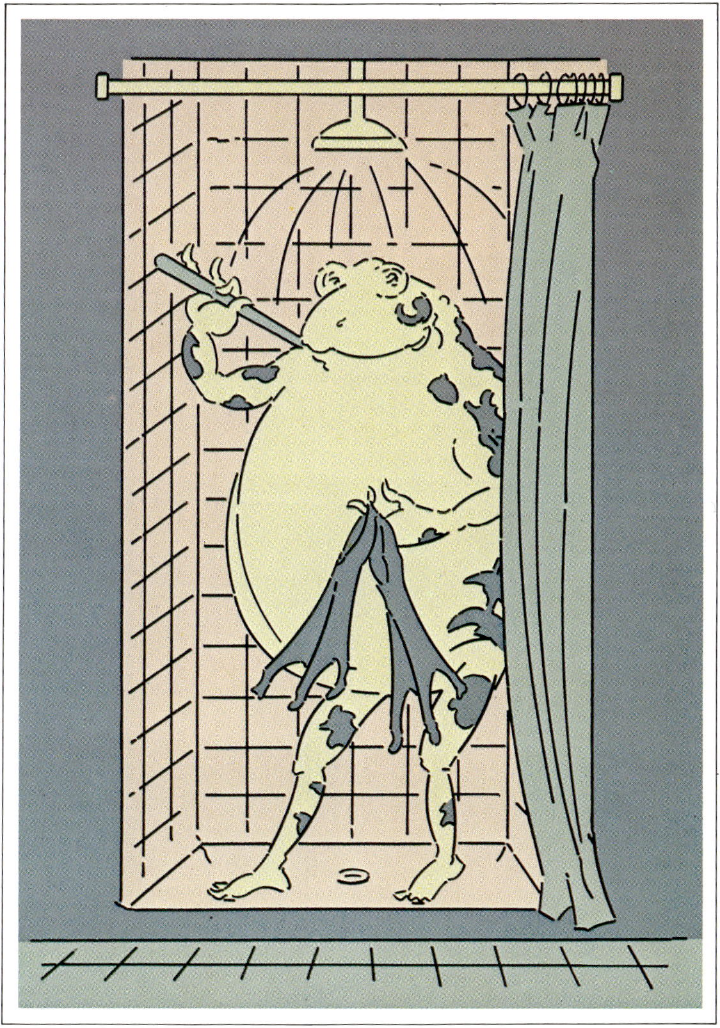

IN PRAISE OF THE FROG

Frogs sit more solid
Than anything sits. In mid-leap they are
Parachutists falling
In a free fall. They die on roads
With arms across their chests and
Heads high.

I love frogs that sit
Like Buddha, that fall without
Parachutes, that die
Like Italian tenors.

Above all, I love them because,
Pursued in water, they never
Panic so much that they fail
To make stylish triangles
With their ballet dancers'
Legs.

                NORMAN MacCAIG

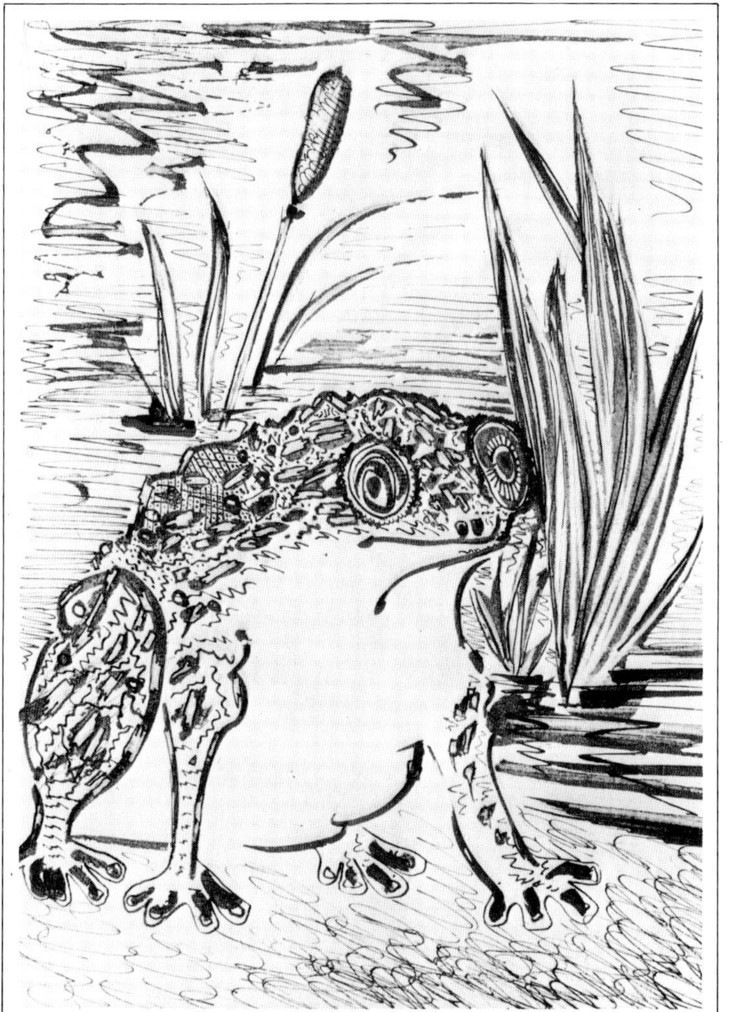

THE ALL-AMERICAN FROG

Frogs have always had a special place in the hearts of Americans. Look at Kermit, the greenest of them all, famous and beloved throughout the world for his sardonic wit and casual crooning, and perpetrator of the international hit-song 'It's not easy being green'.

In 1865 Mark Twain wrote a story called 'The Celebrated Jumping Frog of Calaveras County'. In it he told how a gambler owned a frog who could jump farther than any other, until one day a rival fed him a dose of lead shot and he was grounded on the starting line.

Since that day frog jumping has been a national passion; 1928 saw the first Annual Frog Jumping Championship at Angel's Camp in California's Calaveras County. Today, the contest draws over 20,000 spectators. The winner is the frog who covers the greatest distance in three leaps.

A frog called Budweiser was the contest's first winner. He achieved a total distance of 10 feet, and went on to smash his own record in 1931 and again in 1932, ending with a grand 13 feet 2 inches. He was succeeded by the legendary Maggie, whose record of 16 feet 2 inches remained unbroken for a decade.

In frog jumping the Americans are keen to encourage professionalism. The showman Bill 'Professor' Steed has founded Croaker College, an establishment that trains the elite of frog society in the best American tradition. The student's owners, celebrities such as President Reagan, Dolly Parton and Glen Campbell, pay their bed and board ($65 per term) and provide their charges with a wardrobe of clothes which mirror their own styles.

Frogs having already scored in the worlds of showbusiness and sport, it remains to be seen what challenges their natural good looks and athleticism will lead them to meet next.

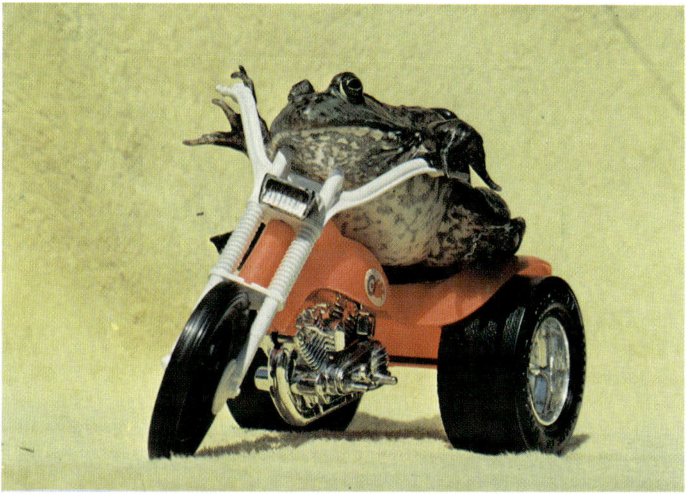

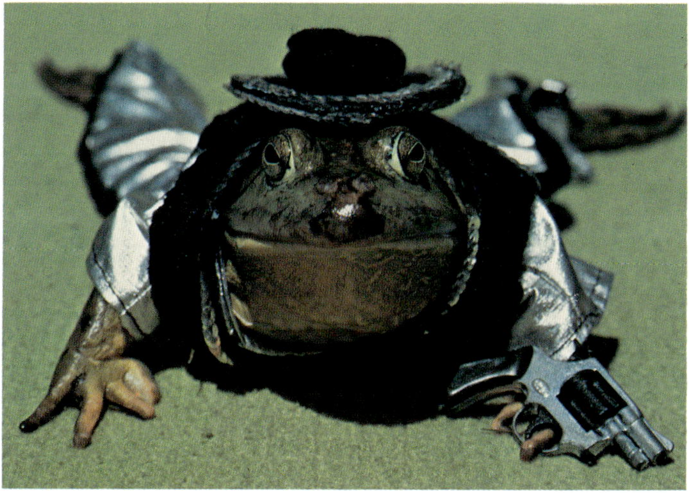

Frog Charms

In folklore, frogs have been found very efficacious in bringing unrequited love to a happy resolution. One charm is believed to ensure you win the man you love. The lovesick girl should stick pins into a frog and put it into a box. When it has died and withered, she should then remove a particular key-shaped bone and sew it secretly into the coat of the man who has caught her fancy. If this cannot be easily done, she can simply place the charm in his pocket. Whichever method is chosen, the following ditty must be recited:

> I do not want to hurt you, frog,
> But my true heart to turn,
> Wishing that he no rest may find,
> Till he come to me and speak his mind.

After a week the man should come to the girl and ask her to marry him.

Another frog charm may bring back an erring lover. It was recorded that a girl whose lover had deserted her stuck needles into a live frog and buried it. Her young man, for no apparent reason, fell ill and was tormented with terrible pains. He returned to the girl hoping that she would nurse him. At this she disinterred the frog, removed the pins and the pains miraculously abated. The couple were reunited and joined in holy matrimony.

Nevertheless, if you cannot find a live frog it is worth looking for a frogstone. These yellow frog-shaped stones are found by lakes and bring their owner good luck.

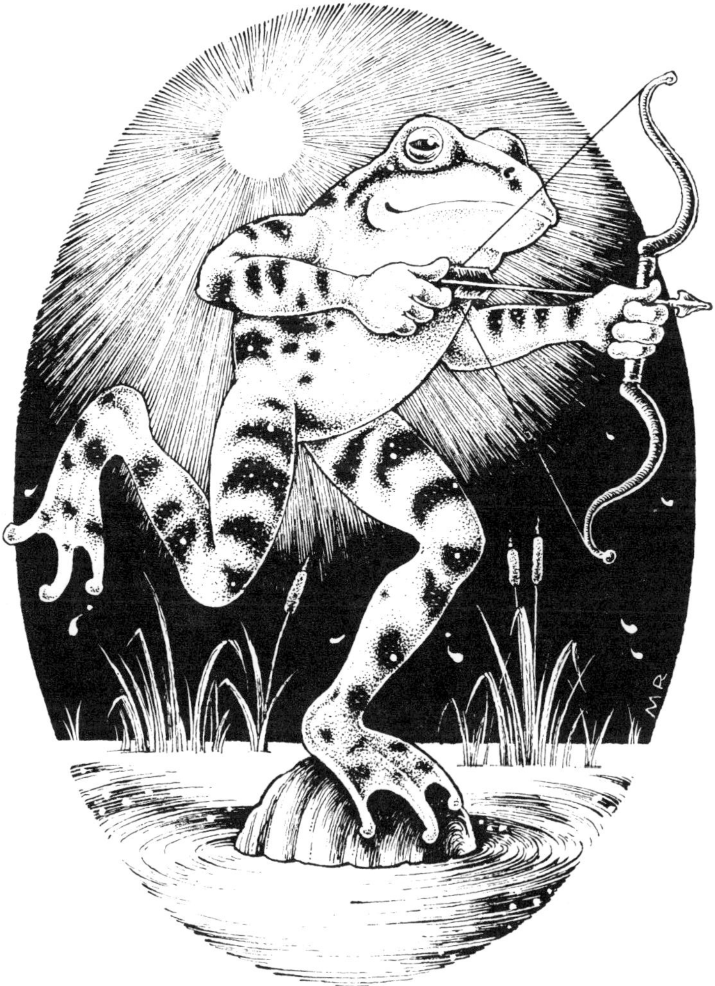

The Useful Frog

A species of South African frog, the plantanna, was until recently used so extensively in pregnancy tests that it became threatened with extinction. To perform the test, 2.5 cc of chemically-treated urine would be injected into the adult female frog. If the woman was pregnant, the frog would lay thousands of eggs within six to twelve hours. If she was not, there would be no eggs. The success rate of this experiment created an enormous demand for the plantanna world-wide, and many South Africans made a living by netting them. In 1962 alone 13,000 frogs were exported to the United States. Luckily for the plantanna, alternative means have now been found for testing.

Frogs can also provide men with deadly weapons. The Cuban arrow poison frog is not only the world's smallest amphibian, with an average length of only 10 mm, but also secretes a deadly venom. The Cuban Indians used to extract this poison and dip their arrow tips into it before shooting at their enemies.

The frog is a very useful pet to keep in any garden, being a good indicator of weather. If its skin is pale yellow, it will be fine, but if it turns a dark greeny-brown, it means rain. The frog is also excellent for pest control because it feeds on insects which devour plants.

It is easy to keep your garden frog content. All it requires is a pond and a mate. It is difficult to keep a frog indoors because it must be fed on live insects, but with perseverance you can tempt one inside by holding small pieces of meat in front of it.

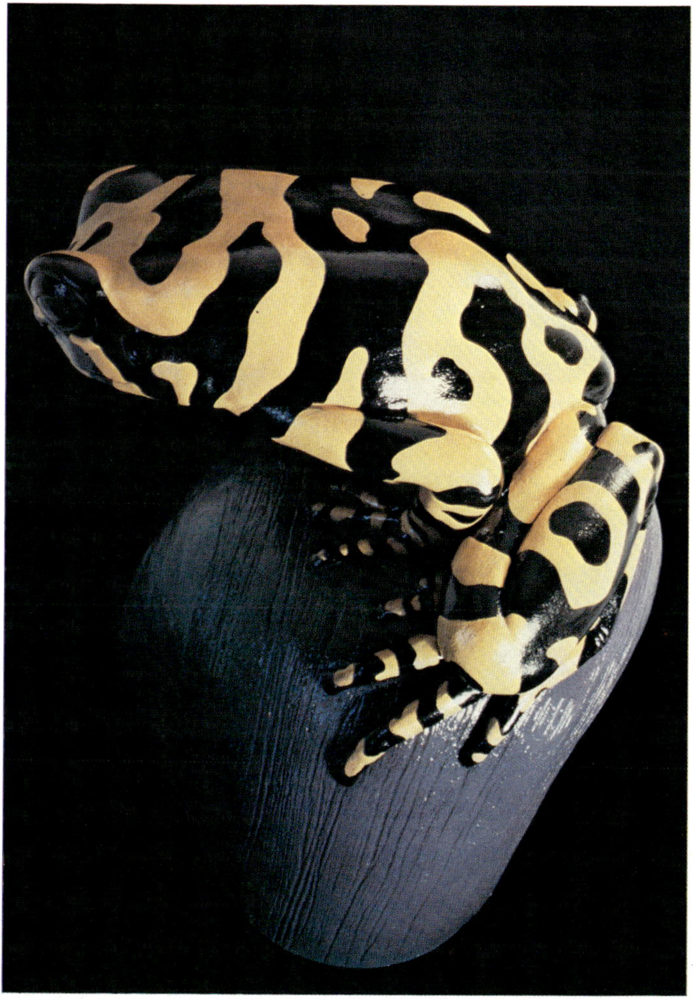

ACKNOWLEDGEMENTS

The author and publishers are grateful for permission to quote copyright passages from the following publications:
'Frogs' from Surroundings by Norman MacCaig (The Hogarth Press); 'The Frog' from Cautionary Tales by Hilaire Belloc (George Duckworth & Co Ltd and Alfred A. Knopf, Inc).

Illustrations
The author and publishers wish to thank the following for permission to reproduce illustrations and photographs: Philip Argent, page 27; Anthony Bennett, pages 11 and 55; British Museum, London, page 9; Bruce Coleman, page 31; Joanna Dickerson, pages 24 and 25; Elgin Court Cards, page 15; EMI, page 41; Mary Evans Picture Library, pages 5, 19, 33 and 35; Camilla Francombe, page 7; Brian Grimwood, page 47; Valerie Hill, pages 21, 36 and 37; Kira Josey, jacket; Mansell Collection, page 29; James Marsh, page 3; New Cavendish Books, page 39; Mark Reddy, page 53; Ann Ronan Picture Library, page 17; Victoria and Albert Museum, page 49; Gillian Weir, page 23; Ian Wright, page 51.

Designed and produced for G.P. Putnam's Sons by
Bellew & Higton Publishers Ltd
19-21 Conway Street, London W1P 6JD
Copyright © Bellew & Higton Publishers Limited 1981
All rights reserved. This book, or parts thereof,
must not be reproduced in any form without permission.
Published on the same day in Canada by Academic Press
Canada Limited, Toronto
Library of Congress Catalog Number 80-84540
ISBN 0 399 12611 2
Printed in England
First American Edition 1981